Steck-Vaughn

Reading Comprehension

Building Vocabulary and Meaning

LEVEL

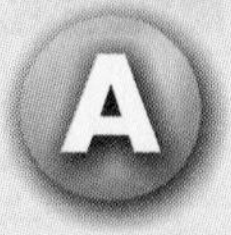

Reviewers

Roberta L. Frenkel
Director of English Language Arts
Community School District 3
New York, New York

Argen Hurley
First Grade Teacher
Ballast Point Elementary
Hillsborough County School District
Tampa, Florida

www.steck-vaughn.com

Contents

Baby Animals

What Do You Already Know?

Think about baby animals you have seen or read about. Tell about them.

Get Ready to Read

As you read, picture each baby animal in your mind. Use your own words to tell about what you read.

A baby duck is a **duckling**.
It has soft feathers.

duckling

A baby kangaroo is a **joey**.
It grows in its mother's pouch.

joey

A baby polar bear is a **cub**.
It is born in a snow den.

A baby crocodile is a **crocklet**.
Its mother holds it in her mouth.

Check Up

Write the correct answer.

cub

duckling

joey

crocklet

1. Which baby grows in its mother's pouch?

2. Which baby is born in a snow den?

3. Which baby has soft feathers?

4. Whose mother holds it in her mouth?

Word Builder

Fill in the circle next to the correct answer.

1. A **duckling** is a baby

○ kangaroo ○ bear

○ crocodile ○ duck

2. A **crocklet** is a baby

○ crocodile ○ bear

○ kangaroo ○ duck

3. A **joey** is a baby

○ kangaroo ○ duck

○ crocodile ○ bear

4. A **cub** is a baby

○ crocodile ○ duck

○ kangaroo ○ bear

Focus Skill

Tell About What You Read

You can use your own words to tell about what you read.

Draw a picture of a baby animal from the story. Write its name on the line.

Your Turn to Write

Write about the baby animal. Use your own words.

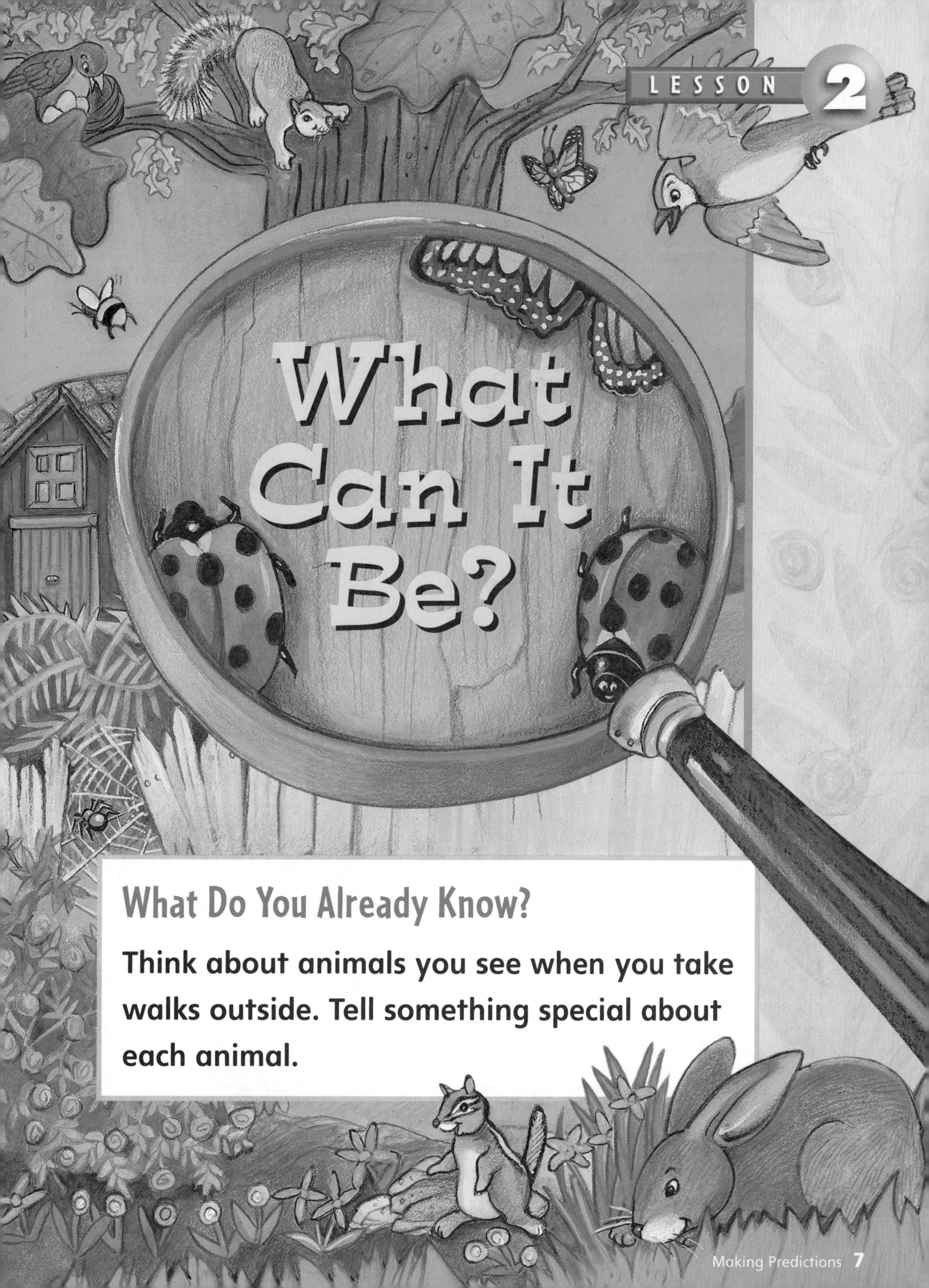

What Can It Be?

What Do You Already Know?

Think about animals you see when you take walks outside. Tell something special about each animal.

Get Ready to Read

As you read, look for picture clues and word clues. Then make a guess about what each animal might be.

This animal is blue.
It has **wings**.
What can it be?

This animal is **gray**.
It is **furry**. What can it be?

It is a blue jay up in a tree.

It is a squirrel
up in a tree.

This animal is black and yellow.
It is **tiny**. It is buzzing.
What can it be?

Check Up

Fill in the circle next to the best answer.

1. Which animal is first in the story?

○ dog

○ blue jay

○ squirrel

○ bear

2. Which animal is second in the story?

○ squirrel

○ mouse

○ cat

○ blue jay

3. This story happens—

○ at home

○ at school

○ on a bus

○ outside

4. The blue jay is in—

○ a tree

○ a lake

○ a barn

○ the grass

Word Builder

▶ **Write the word from the box that tells about each group of animals.**

furry	gray	tiny	wings

1. These animals all have

______________________.

2. These animals are all

______________________.

3. These animals are all

______________________.

4. These animals are all

______________________.

Focus Skill

Make a Guess

You can use word clues and picture clues to make a guess about the story.

Make a guess about the last animal in the story. Draw a picture of it. Write its name on the line.

Your Turn to Write

Think of an animal. Write words to tell how your animal looks.

This animal is ______________________.

It is ______________________.

What can it be? ______________________

LESSON 3

The Stars and Stripes

What Do You Already Know?

Think about our flag. Tell why our flag is important.

Get Ready to Read

As you read, think about what the story is all about. The main idea tells what a story is all about.

The United States **flag** stands for our country and for our people. It is red, white, and blue. It makes us feel **proud**.

Long ago, our country was small. Our flag had 13 **stars** and 13 **stripes**. They stood for the first 13 states.

the first flag

Our country is bigger today. Now our flag has 50 stars. They stand for the 50 states. But our flag still has only 13 stripes.

This map shows the 50 United States.

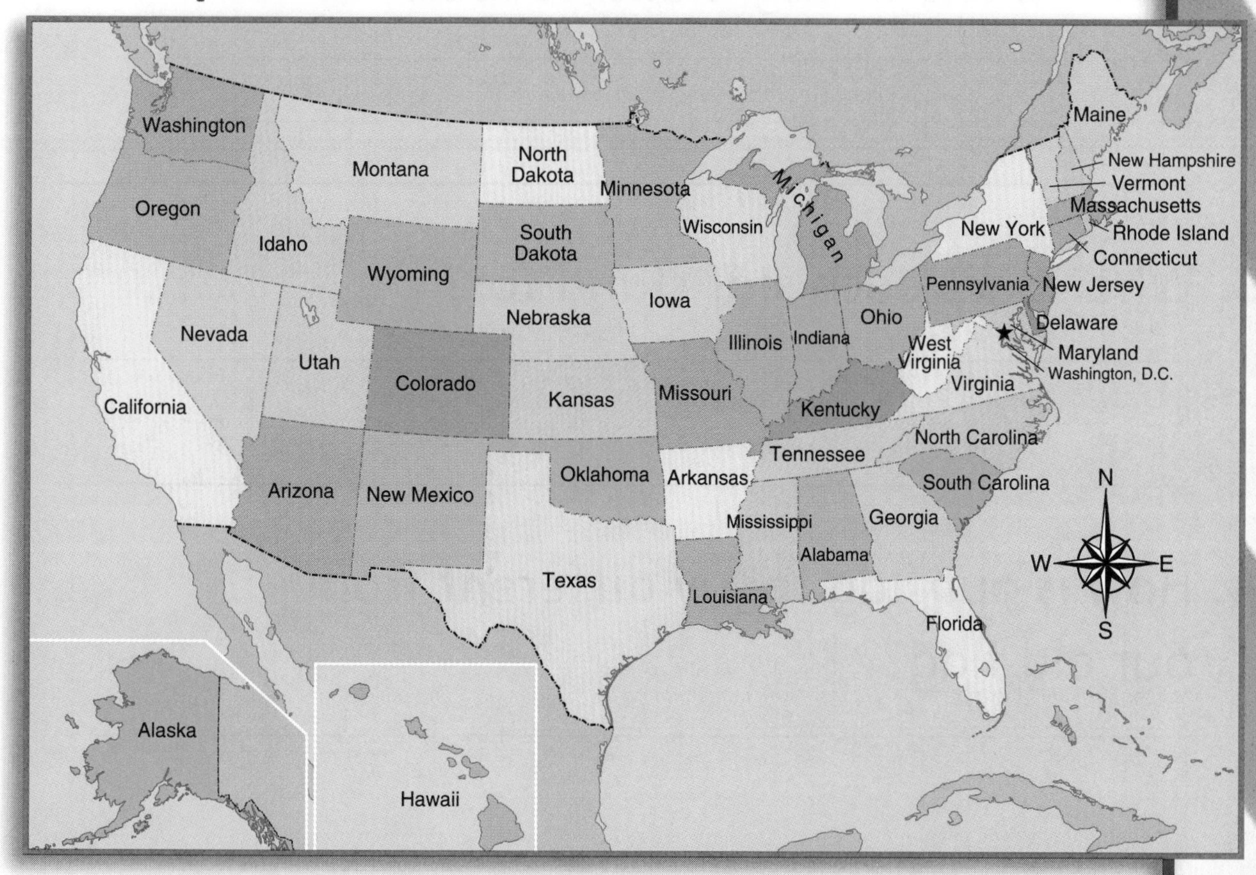

Check Up

Write the correct answer.

1. What does our flag stand for?

2. How does our flag make us feel?

3. What does each star stand for?

4. How is our flag today different from our old flag?

Word Builder

▶ **Fill in the circle next to the best answer.**

1. Our ____ is red, white, and blue.

○ country
○ star
○ people
○ flag

2. They are ____ of our country.

○ proud
○ mad
○ sad
○ silly

3. Our old flag had 13 ____ .

○ colors
○ people
○ stars
○ circles

4. Today our flag has 13 red and white ____ .

○ stars
○ stripes
○ circles
○ colors

Main Idea

The **main idea** tells what a story is **all about.**

▶ Draw a picture to show the main idea of this story.

Your Turn to Write

▶ Write a sentence that tells the main idea of this story.

The Dog and the Bone

What Do You Already Know?

Some make-believe stories are about animals. Do you know a make-believe story about an animal? Tell about it.

Get Ready to Read

Every story has a plot. A plot tells what happens at the beginning, middle, and end of a story. As you read, think about the plot.

One day, Dog went to the **butcher** shop for a **bone**. On the way home, he went over a **bridge**. That is where everything went wrong!

Dog looked into the water. He saw another dog that had a bone. Dog wanted that bone, too.

Dog opened his mouth to get the other bone. Then he jumped at the other dog. Splash! Now Dog had nothing to eat. The water carried away his **dinner**.

Check Up

Fill in the circle next to the best answer.

1. What did Dog have?

○ a book

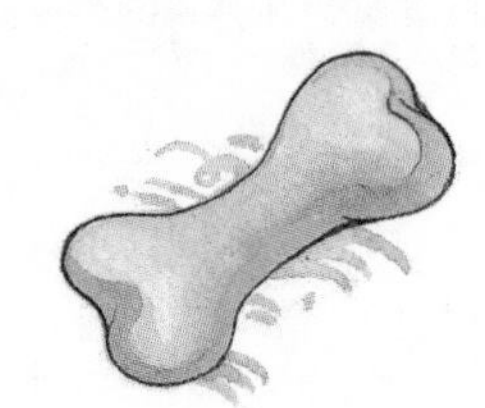

○ a bone

○ a bowl

○ a bag

2. What did Dog want?

○ to swim

○ to fish

○ to play

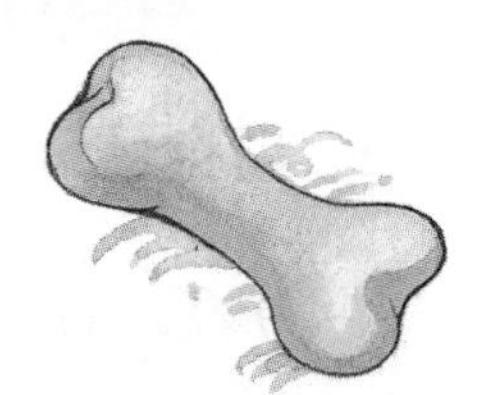

○ another bone

3. Where did Dog lose his bone?

○ his home

○ the butcher

○ the water

○ the park

4. What did Dog really see in the water?

○ himself

○ another dog

○ a fish

○ a boat

Word Builder

▶ **Complete each sentence with a word from the box.**

bone	bridge	butcher	dinner

1. Dog went to the ________________ shop.

2. Dog went over the ________________.

3. Dog wanted the other ________________.

4. Now what will Dog eat for ________________?

Focus Skill

Plot

The **plot** tells what happens in the beginning, middle, and end of a story.

▶ **Write 1, 2, or 3 under each picture to show what happens to Dog in the story.**

Your Turn to Write

▶ **Write some sentences to tell what happens in the beginning, middle, and end of this story.**

The Life of a Frog

What Do You Already Know?

Have you ever seen a frog? Do you know how a frog changes as it grows?

Get Ready to Read

As you read, think about the changes that happen to a frog. Think about the order in which the changes happen.

First, frogs lay their eggs in a pond. A pond is a good place because the water moves very little. Next, the eggs **hatch**. Then the young frogs eat food that they find in the pond.

A young frog is a **tadpole**. It swims like a fish. It has **gills** so it can **breathe** like a fish, too.

Then, a tadpole changes as it grows. It grows legs. Its gills go away. It loses its tail. At last, it is a frog.

Check Up

Write the correct answer.

1. Where do frogs lay their eggs?

2. What happens after the eggs hatch?

3. How is a young frog like a fish?

4. What is one way a frog changes as it grows?

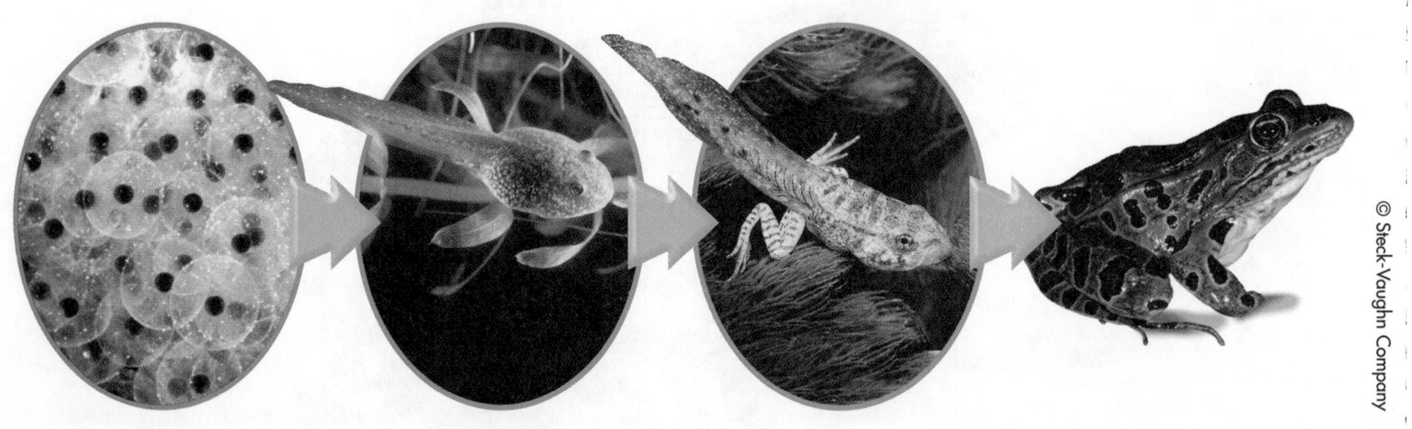

Word Builder

Fill in the circle next to the correct answer.

1. A young frog is called a ____.

○ bird

○ tadpole

○ turtle

○ cat

2. A tadpole has ____ like a fish.

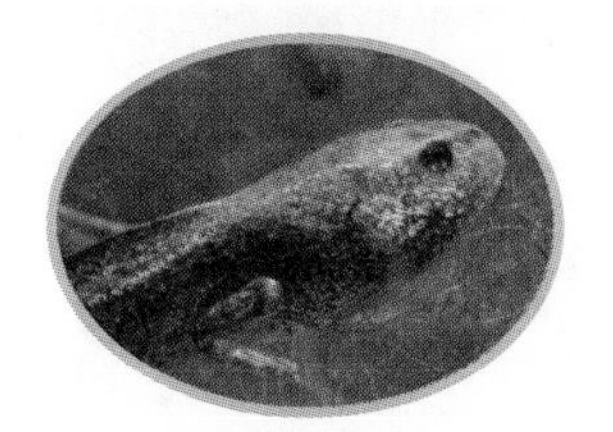

○ gills

○ legs

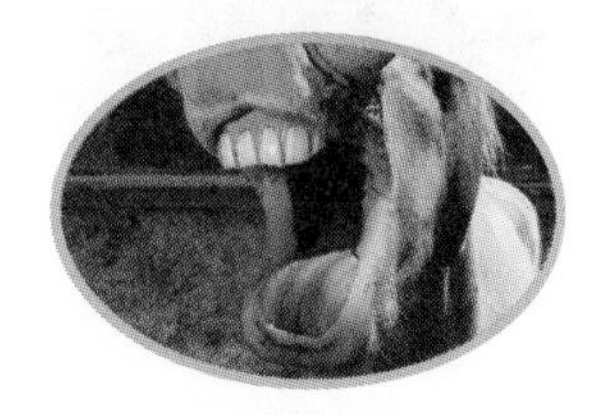

○ teeth

○ wings

3. A tadpole uses gills to ____.

○ swim

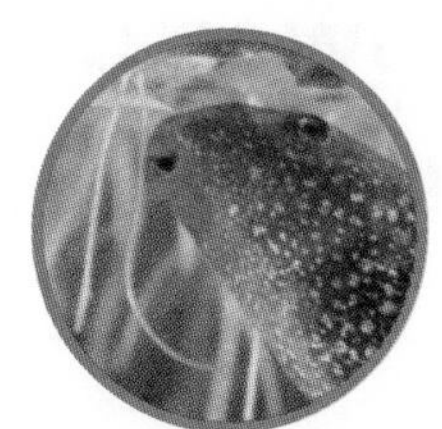

○ eat

○ breathe

○ jump

4. After a frog lays its eggs, the eggs ____.

○ jump

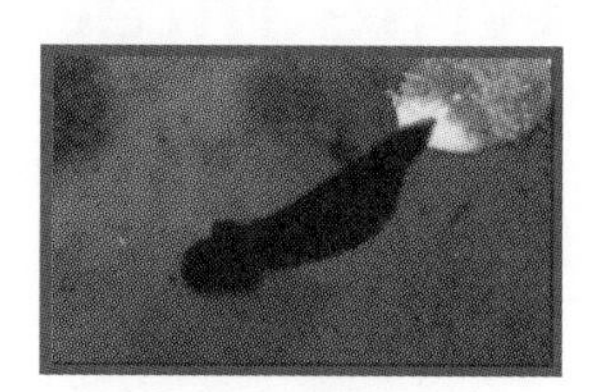

○ hatch

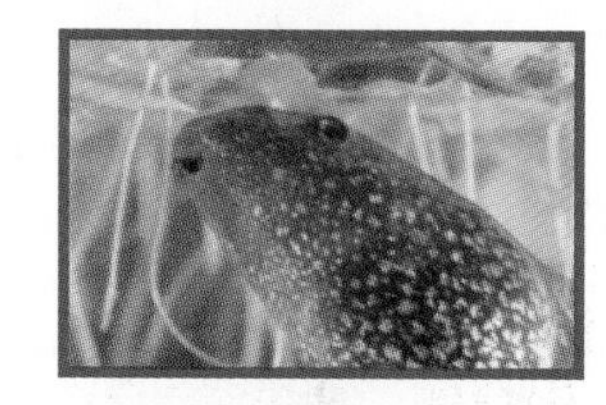

○ eat

○ swim

Focus Skill

Sequence

You can tell about the changes in a story in the order that they happen.

▶ **Write 1, 2, 3, or 4 under each picture to show the order of how a frog grows.**

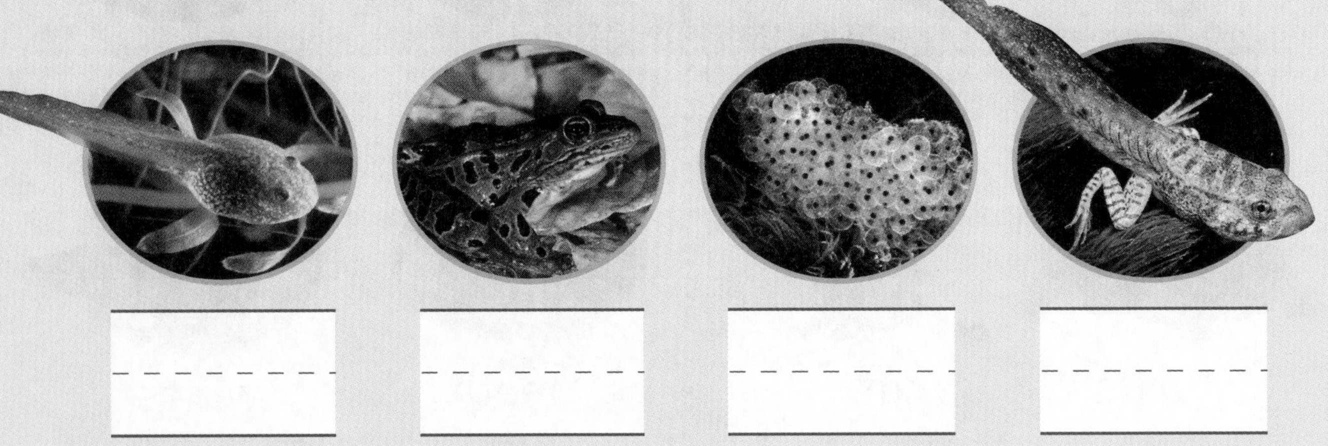

Your Turn to Write

▶ **Write three sentences about how you get ready for school. Use words such as first, next, and last.**

REVIEW

A Pet for Ana

"I see the pet I want," said Ana.
"It is not too small. It is not too big.
It is white with spots. It has a short tail.
It has long ears. It does not meow."

Dad said, "We need to think of a name!"

Fill in the circle next to the best answer.

1. What will Ana get?

○ fish

○ kitten

○ puppy

○ rabbit

2. Who is with Ana?

○ Mom

○ Grandpa

○ Sister

○ Dad

Time to Grow!

You can grow a plant. Put a seed in soil. Give it water and light. Soon it will start to grow. First, the seed grows a root. Next, the seed grows a stem and leaves. Then the stem grows taller. Last, it becomes a grown plant!

Fill in the circle next to the best answer.

1. What happens after a seed grows a root?

- ○ It grows a stem and leaves.
- ○ You put it in soil.
- ○ It becomes a grown plant.
- ○ You give it water.

2. What is another good title for this story?

- ○ Plants and Animals
- ○ Growing Stems
- ○ Water the Plant
- ○ You Can Grow a Plant

6

Insects

What Do You Already Know?

Do you like insects? Which insects can you name? Tell what you know about them.

Get Ready to Read

As you read, think about how all insects are the same. Think about how they are different.

How are all insects the same? All insects have six **legs**. All have three **body** parts. All have two **feelers** on their heads.

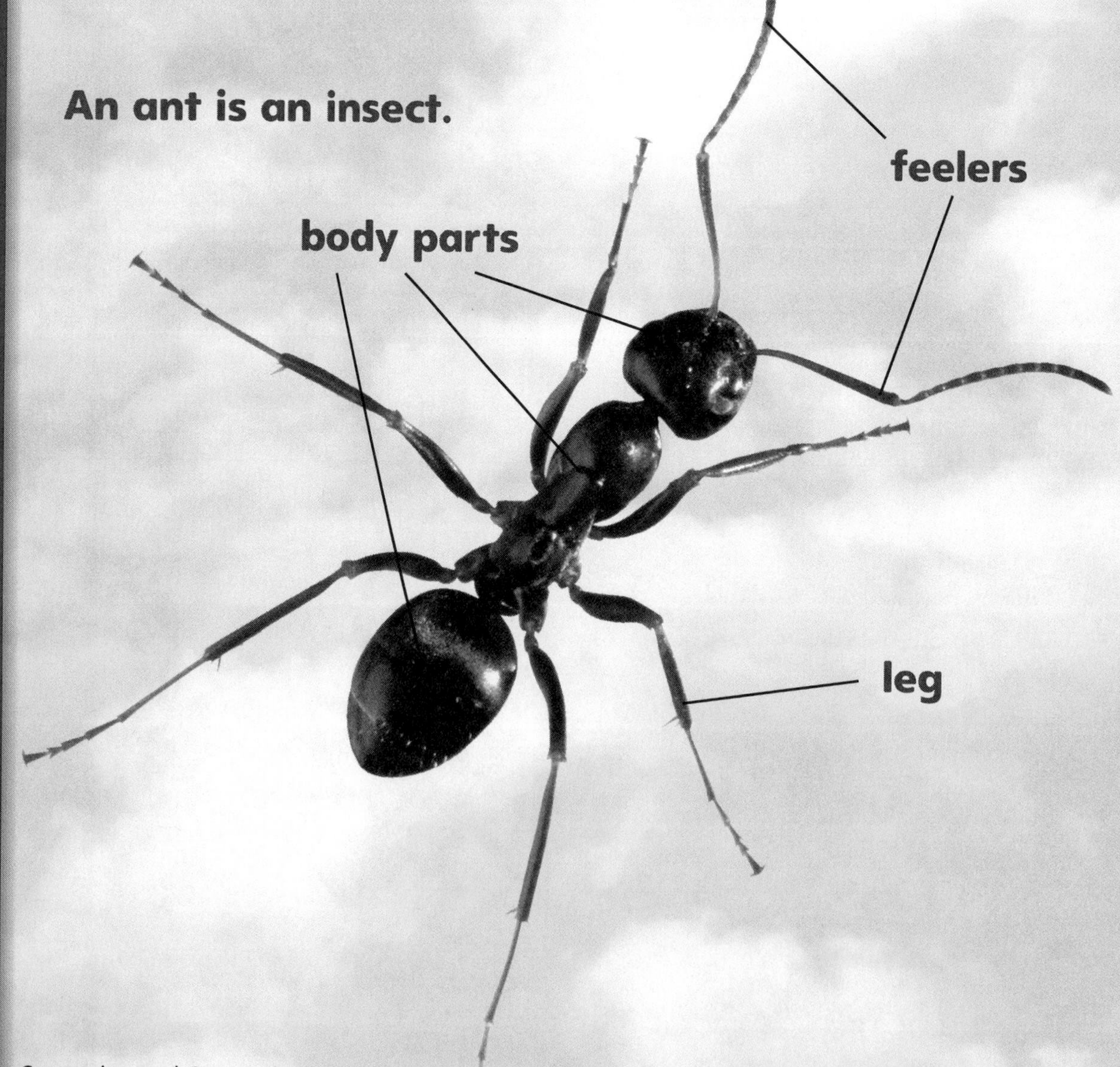

An ant is an insect.

All insects hatch from eggs.
Young insects eat all the time.

insect eggs

Soon young insects grow up.
Then they may look very different.

Many insects have wings. A bee has small wings. Some moths have very big wings.

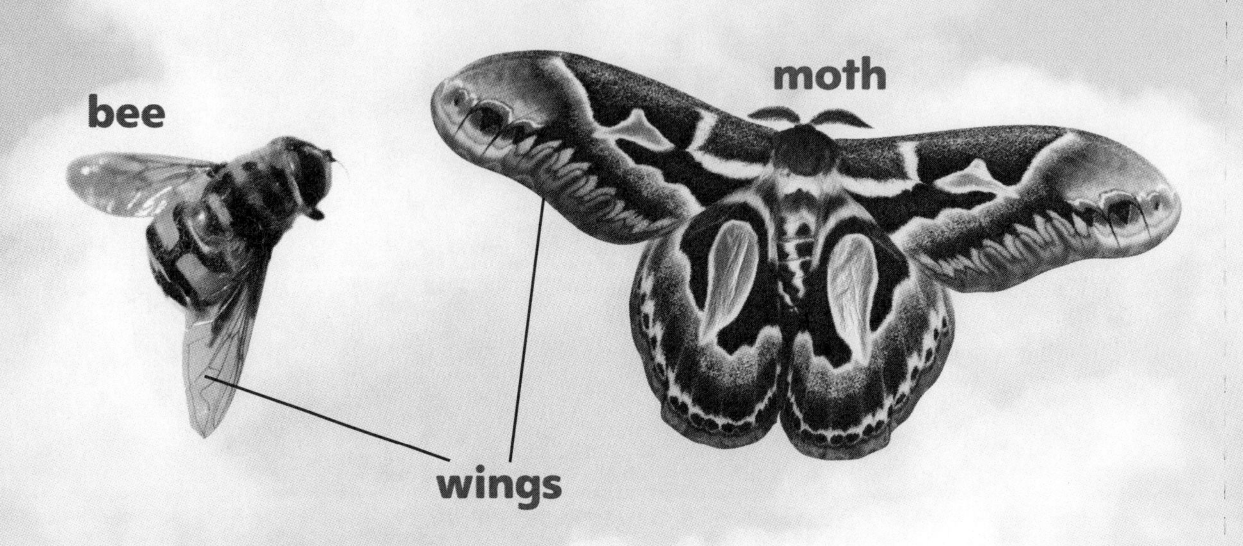

How are insects different? Insects come in many different colors. They move in different ways. Different insects can **climb** or fly. Some can jump or swim.

Check Up

Fill in the circle next to the correct answer.

1. How many legs do all insects have?

○ two ○ three

○ four ○ six

2. What does every insect have?

○ feelers ○ a beak

○ a big head ○ a tail

3. What do young insects do all the time?

○ fly ○ eat

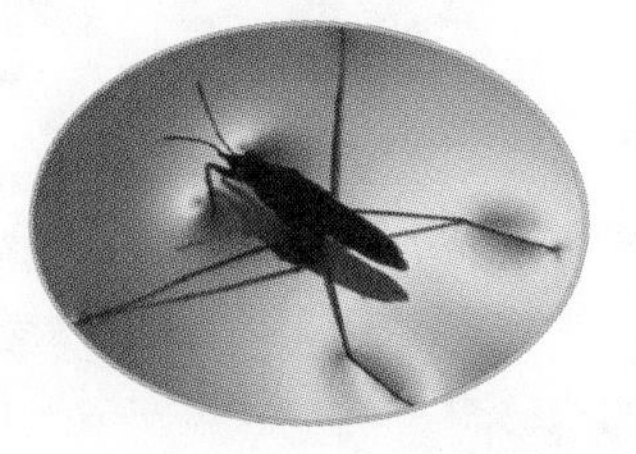

○ swim ○ jump

4. Which of these insects has the biggest wings?

○ bee ○ moth

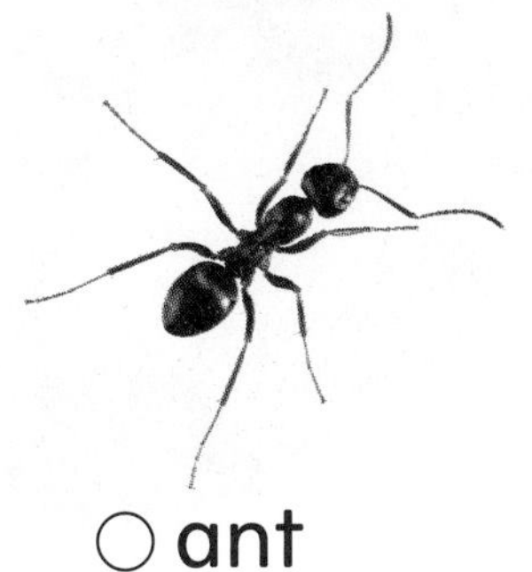

○ fly ○ ant

Word Builder

▶ **Choose a word from the box to complete each sentence. Write it on the line.**

body	**climb**	**feelers**	**legs**

1. Insects have two ____________.

2. Insects have three ____________ parts.

3. Insects have six ____________.

4. Some insects can jump or ____________.

Same and Different

You can tell how things are the **same**.
You can also tell how things are **different**.

▶ For each row, write X in the correct box.
Show how insects are the same.
Show how insects can be different.

Insects	Same	Different
1. color		X
2. 3 body parts		
3. 6 legs		
4. wings		
5. how they move		

Your Turn to Write

For each row, write X in the correct box. Show how the cat and dog are the same. Show how they are different.

Cat and Dog	Same	Different
1. size		
2. color		
3. 4 legs		
4. tail		

Write two sentences about cats and dogs. Tell how they are the same. Tell how they are different.

LESSON 7

The Other Story of the Three Bears

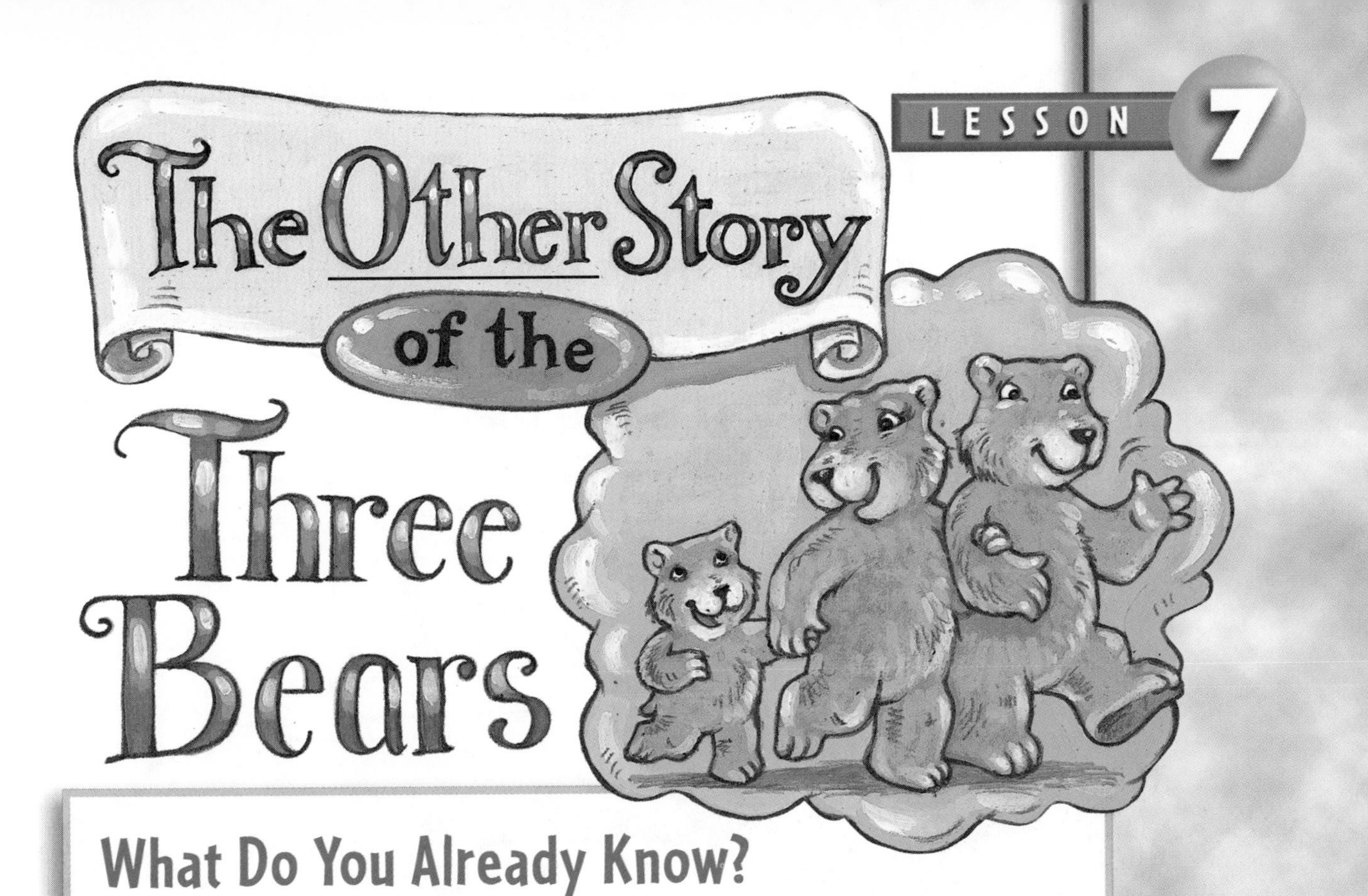

What Do You Already Know?

Do you know the story of the Three Bears? Use the pictures on this page to help you tell the story.

Get Ready to Read

As you read, think about the place where this other story happens. Think about what it is like there.

One day the three bears went for a walk. They came to the house where a girl lived. No one was home. They went in.

"What a pretty house!" they said.

Mama Bear found three hats. The first hat was too big. The second hat was too small. But the third hat was just right!

Papa Bear found three cakes. The first cake was too **sweet**. The second cake was too **dry**. But the third cake was just right!

Baby Bear found three chairs. The first chair was too **hard**. The second chair was too **soft**. But the third chair was just right!

The three bears went home. Then they saw a girl run out of their house. "That girl was in our house!" said Papa Bear.

"You should not go into someone else's house!" said Mama Bear.

"It is just not right!" said Baby Bear.

Check Up

Write the answer to each question.

1. What did Papa Bear find?

2. What did Baby Bear find?

3. Where did the bears go last?

4. Who did the bears see run away?

Word Builder

Read each underlined word. Fill in the circle next to the words that mean the same thing.

1. One cake was <u>dry</u>.
   - ○ not wet
   - ○ very warm
   - ○ too yellow
   - ○ not tall

2. One chair was <u>hard</u>.
   - ○ too small
   - ○ too hot
   - ○ not red
   - ○ not soft

3. One chair was <u>soft</u>.
   - ○ very cold
   - ○ not hard
   - ○ not blue
   - ○ too big

4. One cake was too <u>sweet</u>.
   - ○ tastes good
   - ○ tastes hot
   - ○ tastes bad
   - ○ tastes cold

Place

The place is where a story happens.

Draw a picture of the house where the girl in the story lives. Write words to tell about it.

Your Turn to Write

Think of a story you know. Then draw a picture to show where the story happens.

Write one sentence to tell where the story happens. Use describing words in your sentence.

Take Care of Yourself!

LESSON 8

What Do You Already Know?

What do you do to take good care of yourself? Tell what you do.

Get Ready to Read

As you read, you can learn what happens. You can also learn why it happens.

Exercise makes you strong.

Why should you exercise?

Exercise makes your body strong. A strong body helps you work and play. A strong body does not get sick easily. Exercise to help keep your body **healthy**.

Why should you eat right?

Your body needs **vitamins**. Vitamins help you grow and stay strong. Fruits and vegetables have many vitamins. Eat good foods to stay healthy.

Fruits and vegetables have many vitamins.

Why should you keep clean?

Germs are all over. Germs can make you sick. Soap and warm water help kill germs. Stay clean to stay healthy.

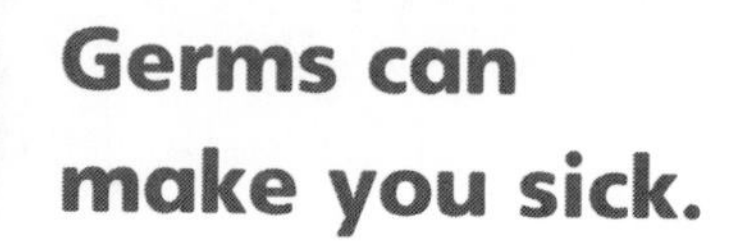

Germs can make you sick.

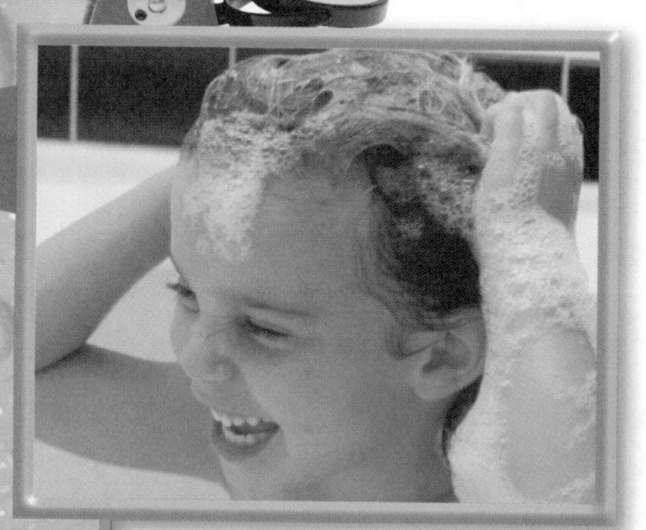

Check Up

Fill in the circle next to the best answer.

1. Stay healthy and take care of your—

- ○ soap
- ○ food
- ○ body
- ○ vitamins

2. Exercise keeps you—

- ○ strong
- ○ tired
- ○ clean
- ○ warm

3. You can eat good foods to get—

- ○ exercise
- ○ vitamins
- ○ germs
- ○ soap

4. What can kill germs?

- ○ exercise
- ○ vitamins
- ○ soap and water
- ○ fruits and vegetables

Word Builder

▶ **Complete each sentence with a word from the box. Write the word on the line.**

exercise	germs	healthy	vitamins

1. You can get sick from ____.

2. Running is good ____.

3. Fruits have many ____.

4. Eating right helps keep you ____.

Focus Skill

What and Why

You can learn **what** happens. You can also learn **why** it happens.

▶ Write the words to complete the chart.

germs   strong   healthy

Why Something Happens	What Happens
If you wash with soap and water—	then you kill ________________.
If you exercise—	then your body gets ________________.
If you eat right—	then you stay ________________.

Your Turn to Write

Think of a way you take care of yourself. Write what you do. Then write what happens.

Why It Happens	What Happens
If I—	then I—

Write two sentences to tell how you take care of yourself. Use your chart.

Sam and Bob

What Do You Already Know?

Think of a story that has make-believe animals or people. Tell what they looked like. Then tell what they did in the story.

Get Ready to Read

As you read, think about what parts of the story could happen in real life. Think about what parts could not really happen.

One **night** something woke up Sam. A little monster stood by him.

"I am going to live under your bed," it said.

Sam said, "You will be cold there. You can live in my **closet**."

Sam and the monster became **friends**. Sam named the monster Bob.

It was nice to have Bob as a friend. Bob played games with Sam. Bob also helped Sam with his **homework**.

Sam's friend Dan came to stay one night. "What did I hear?" Dan asked. "Is something under your bed?"

Sam said, "Nothing is under my bed. But my monster is in the closet."

"M-m-monster?" asked Dan.

Sam said, "Don't be scared. You can meet him! His name is Bob."

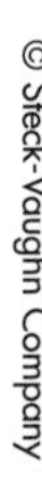

Check Up

Write the correct answer for each question.

1. Who wanted to live under Sam's bed?

2. Where did the monster want to sleep first?

3. What was it like under Sam's bed?

4. What did Bob and Sam play?

Word Builder

▶ **Fill in the circle next to the best answer.**

1. People who have fun together are—

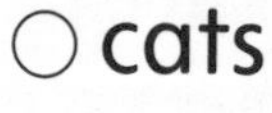

○ cats ○ friends

○ monsters ○ bears

2. You keep clothes in the—

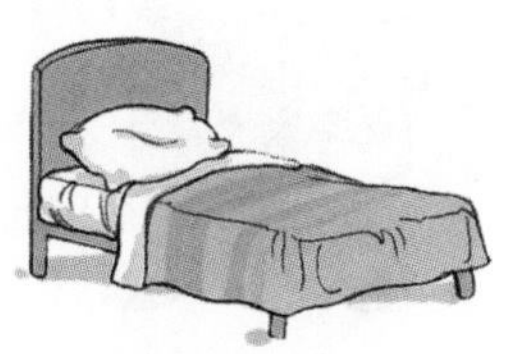

○ table ○ bed

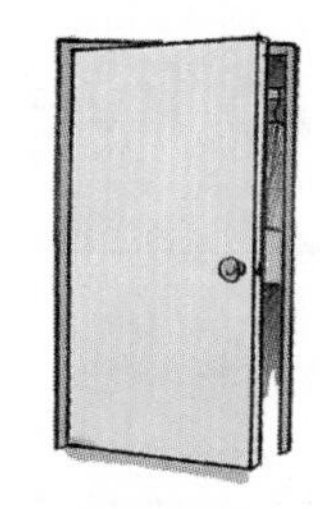

○ closet ○ chair

---

3. The moon comes out at—

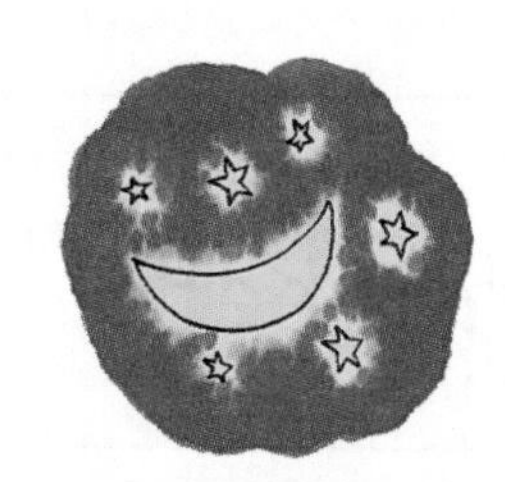

○ day ○ night

○ noon ○ winter

4. After school, you may do your math—

○ homework ○ lunch

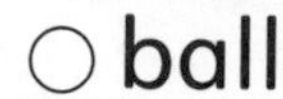

○ ball ○ dishes

Focus Skill

Real or Not Real

Some things that happen in stories could happen in real life. Some things could not really happen.

Mark an X to show if each thing could happen in real life or could not really happen.

What Happens in the Story	Could Happen	Could Not Happen
A boy sleeps in a bed.	X	
A monster sleeps in a closet.		X
A boy does his homework.		
A monster helps a boy do his homework.		
A boy stays at a friend's house.		

Your Turn to Write

- Think of a story about a make-believe friend. Draw something that could happen in real life. Draw something that could not really happen.

Could Happen	Could Not Happen

- Write two sentences about your make-believe friend. Use your chart.

Holidays!

LESSON 10

What Do You Already Know?

Which holidays do you like best?
What do you do on these holidays?

Get Ready to Read

The main idea is what a story is all about. As you read, look for details that tell who, what, when, and where.

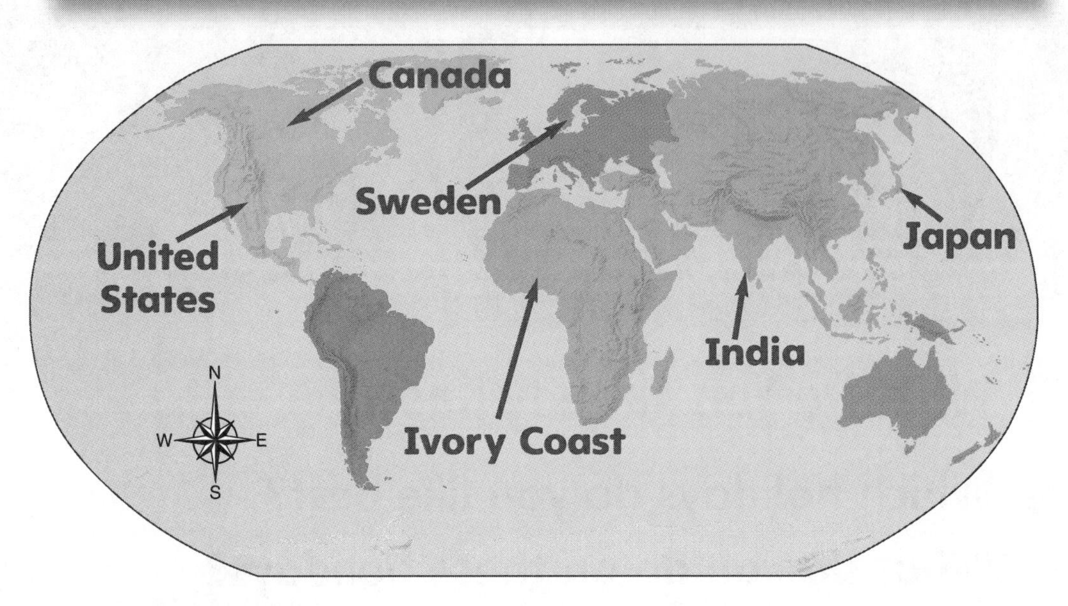

Holidays take place at any time of the year. They take place all over the **world**.

Many **countries** have holidays in fall. In Ivory Coast, people dress up and dance on this holiday.

In winter, some countries have a snow holiday. People make ice art on this snow holiday in Japan.

Canada also has a snow holiday. People make ice art there, too. They also have ice races.

This spring holiday is in India. People there throw colored powder into the air.

In summer, some people in Sweden **celebrate** the longest day of the year. They dress in costumes and play music.

Check Up

Fill in the circle next to the best answer.

1. What do people do on snow holidays?

- ○ make ice art
- ○ dress up
- ○ dance
- ○ throw colored powder

2. When do people celebrate holidays?

- ○ only in winter
- ○ only in summer
- ○ only in spring
- ○ any time of year

3. Where do people throw colored powder on a holiday?

- ○ Japan
- ○ India
- ○ Canada
- ○ Sweden

4. Why do some people celebrate in summer?

- ○ because it is hot
- ○ because it is cold
- ○ because it has the longest day
- ○ because it has the shortest day

Word Builder

Read each clue. Then write the word it tells about.

celebrate	countries	holidays	world

1. This is made of land and water.

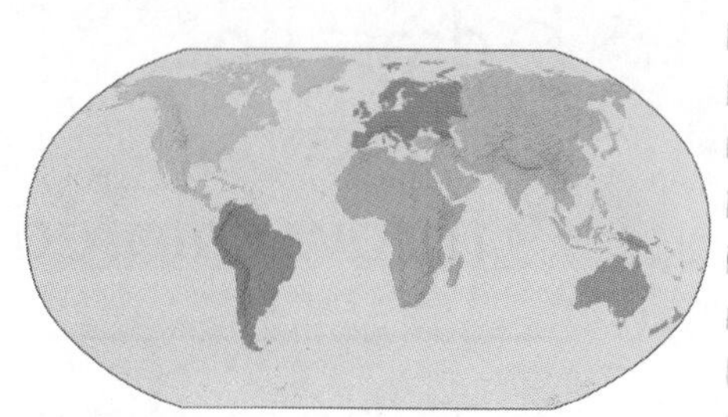

2. These are special times of the year.

3. We like to do this on holidays.

4. You can find them on a map.

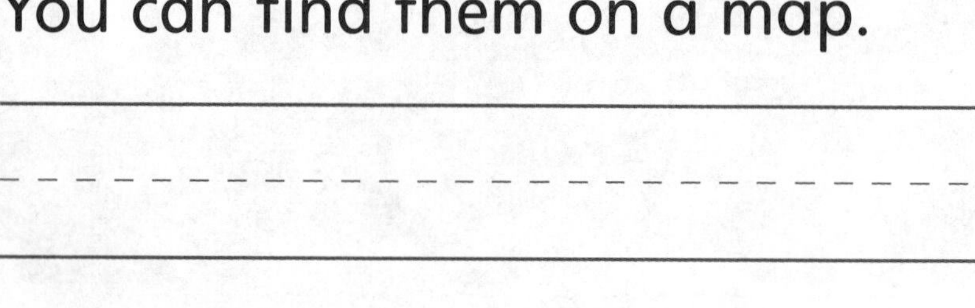

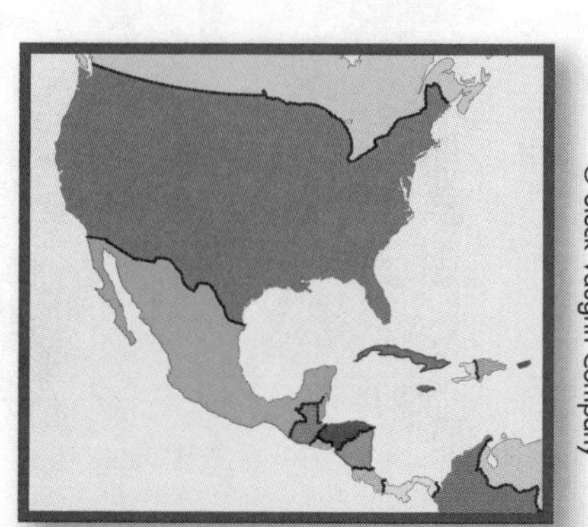

Main Idea and Details

The **main idea** is what a story is about.

Details tell **who**, **what**, **when**, and **where**.

▶ Complete this chart. Write an answer on each line.

Main Idea	People celebrate holidays.
Who celebrates?	people all over the world
What do they do?	
When do they celebrate?	
Where do they celebrate?	

Your Turn to Write

Write in the chart about your favorite holiday.

Main Idea	My favorite holiday is ______________.
Who celebrates?	
What do you celebrate?	
When do you celebrate?	
Where do you celebrate?	

Write two sentences that tell how you celebrate.

How the Fly Got Its Color

A Folktale

Long ago, some insects played in a garden. They jumped over a mud puddle. They would not let Red Fly play.

"Flies do not jump well," said Cricket.

Red Fly jumped anyway. He fell in the puddle and was covered in black mud. That is why flies are black today.

Fill in the circle next to the best answer.

1. Where does this story happen?

- ○ At the beach
- ○ In a garden
- ○ In a school
- ○ In a house

2. What could not really happen?

- ○ A fly could not be black.
- ○ A cricket could not talk.
- ○ Insects could not be in a garden.
- ○ A fly could not be near mud.

What a Katydid Does

The way a katydid looks helps keep it safe. It looks like a part of a plant. This makes it hard for birds to see it.

Sometimes katydids call out to other katydids. They do not use their mouths like people do. They rub their legs together to make noise.

▶ **Fill in the circle next to the best answer.**

1. The katydid is hard for birds to see because ____.

○ it is so small
○ it looks like a plant
○ it hides under the ground
○ it rubs its legs together

▶ **Write the correct answer.**

2. How are katydids different from people?

____

____

Glossary

body
Ants have three **body** parts.

bone

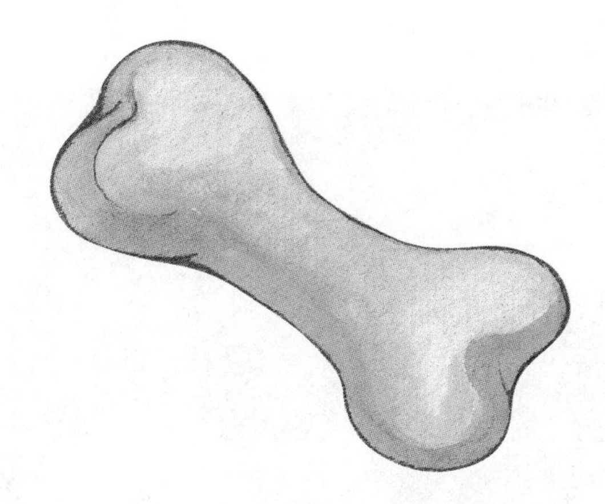

The dog ate the **bone**.

breathe
Tadpoles **breathe** like fish.

bridge
The **bridge** goes over the river.

butcher
The **butcher** sells meat.

celebrate
We **celebrate** many holidays.

climb
An ant can **climb** up a tree.

closet
Put your coat in the **closet**.

countries
All **countries** have their own flag.

crocklet
A baby crocodile is a **crocklet**.

cub

A baby polar bear is a **cub**.

Dd

dinner

The dog had a bone for **dinner**.

dry

Papa Bear thought the cake was too **dry**.

duckling

A baby duck is a **duckling**.

exercise

You should **exercise** every day.

feelers

An ant has two **feelers** on its head.

flag

The girl waves the **flag**.

friends

Two **friends** play together.

furry

A squirrel has a **furry** tail.

germs

Wash your hands to kill **germs**.

gills

A tadpole uses **gills** to breathe.

gray

A squirrel has **gray** fur.

hard

Baby Bear thought one chair was too **hard**.

hatch

Crocklets **hatch** from eggs.

healthy

Stay clean to stay **healthy**.

holidays

We have fun on **holidays**.

homework

Sam's teacher gave him **homework**.

Jj

joey

A baby kangaroo is a **joey**.

legs

Insects have six **legs**.

night

Sam goes to bed at **night**.

proud

I am **proud** of my good grades.

soft

Baby Bear thought one chair was too **soft**.

stars

Our flag has fifty **stars**.

stripes

Our flag has red and white **stripes**.

sweet

Candy is **sweet**.

tadpole

A **tadpole** is a young frog.

tiny

Bees are **tiny** animals.

vitamins

Foods with **vitamins** help you grow strong.

wings

A bird has two **wings**.

world

We took a trip around the **world**.